With Hope
Comes Peace

I0104281

Helen Care

chipmunkapublishing
the mental health publisher

Published by
Chipmunkapublishing
PO Box 6872
Brentwood
Essex CM13 1ZT
United Kingdom

http://www.chipmunkapublishing.com

Copyright © Helen Care 2012

Edited by Aleks Lech

ISBN   978-1-84991-760-5

Chipmunkapublishing gratefully acknowledge the support of Arts Council England.

Foreword by Jem Price

Helen died at home in December 2011. It seems that her reserves of hope had run dry. I dearly wish that Helen was still with us but know that she has now found some kind of peace. Helen had read and approved the Foreword which follows. Indeed, she had sent the entire manuscript to her publisher and was really pleased that it had been accepted for publication. I suppose that I could have gone through this Foreword, changing 'is' to 'was' but I like to think that Helen still 'is'. So, this is for you, Helen. Cheers, my dear.

I've known Helen longer than pretty much anyone else. I knew Helen before she was mad – or at least before she let people know she was mad. I knew Helen before all those professionals (caring and uncaring) whose crazy-paving she's crossed. Anyway, the point is that I know Helen pretty well because she's an old mate of mine. And yet I've learnt much more about her from these poems.

Helen's first book was called 'With Anger Comes Hope' but I think this collection actually conveys that anger even more effectively. Here, she is externalising her anger, voicing it, almost naming names. Screaming at the *real* sinners (they know who they are); swearing at the insecurities and struggles *they* left her with; sharing something of the fucking awful nightmares that *they* caused. As you may be able to tell, it makes me pretty angry too, on the quiet.

I think Helen thinks too much. I think I understand why she thinks as much as she does but I hope that one day her head will be uncluttered by thoughts of goodness and evil, of perfect love and feared-rejection, of life and death. There are some one-syllable themes in this book that most of us should be able to relate to: love, lies, loss, fear, drink, drugs. Given the subject matter, I found some surprisingly helpful hints among these pages. Helen's words are matter of fact because they *are* a matter of fact. This book isn't a laugh - but you do need to know that Helen is thoughtful and gifted and very funny.

Talking of being funny, people overuse exclamation marks. It irritates me. Then again, I get annoyed when people ask if they can 'get' a latte. Helen also uses exclamation marks - but she uses them appropriately, not just to say 'Laugh Now'. Helen *exclaims* - and she has good reason to. When she's been having a particularly difficult time, I've often exhorted Helen to seek solace in the wise words, popularised by Ronan Keating: "Life is a rollercoaster, just gotta ride it". Ok, fasten your safety harness!!!

Mystery Explained

Bleed because I'm angry
Bleed because I'm sad
Bleed because I'm crazy
Bleed because I'm bad

Bleed because you hate me
Bleed because you don't
Bleed because you love me
Bleed because I won't

Bleed because you left me
Bleed because you stayed
Bleed because you stained me
Bleed because you strayed

Bleed because I'm sorry
Bleed because I'll mend
Bleed because eventually
We're parted in the end.

H.C. 05/04/2009

Be Less Tension

Feeling suicidal is like Catch - 22
Making emotions just like you do
Please be upfront with this experience
I feel alone in mine you're a hindrance

Your response was anger and then shame
I am embarrassed so I take the blame
You were part of making me afraid
Pushing me to the edge, now who is brave?

I need you to be honest, I need you to connect
Without casting blame that you'll detect
You make me feel crazy, you make me feel nervous
Now I feel so numb, if I feel then I'm unconscious!

I feel so scared, I feel so very hurt
I feel concerned, now I'm on the alert
Take off the defensive that makes me small
Your smile I admire, I feel ten feet tall

I'll find my avenues that'll lead to expression
Get it out, let it out, find my confusion
Vent your anger and fear, scream out in frustration
If you can do this there'll be less tension.

H.C.   20/08/2009

Secrets Are Deadly

Secrets underlie suicidal thoughts
I can't easily recall these memories
I speak only of the crisis at hand
Bury me as well as my vulnerabilities

Discount trauma, keep my chin up!
Look on the bright side attitude
But this can lead to fear and shame
Making it difficult to find platitude

Difficult feelings make it hard to give
Don't feel like I can ask for support
Secrets are deadly, they can kill
Suicidal thoughts I always fought

I need an outlet for the turmoil
That's eating away at my soul
Please can you give me peace of mind
So I can gather myself up and become whole

Secrets underlie suicidal thoughts
That take over your personality
For this cycle needs to be broken
Interrupt my fantasy that is my reality.

H.C. 21/08/2009

"If The Core Of

You Is Happy,

Then The Rest

Of You Can Be

Happy Too!"

H.C. 10/05/2009

I Need To Talk

I need to talk, stop
Whatever you're doing
Turn off the television
Put down your book
Tell me you're there
For me without confusion

Look me straight in the eye
Nod your head to me
If I start to cry
Allow my tears to roll
I need to feel sad
Until my tears run dry

Breathe deeply as I share
Your discomfort will rise
Take a sip of water
To help keep your attention
Look at me with compassion
For I was once a daughter

Breathe to keep your equilibrium
Let your anger out later
Go for a drive and scream
Tell me that you love me
Draw close and hold my hand
I need to talk, but what does this all mean?

H.C. 21/08/2009

Getting Something Right

I think it slightly nouveau riche-esque and middle class
This was my only responsibility, I'll get pissed and have
a laugh
I admitted to being Borderline, of what I hear you ask,
not as
A drinker or partaker of drugs, but in personality, such a
task.

Everybody should kill themselves, I am fine with that –
aren't you?
I would've been more fraught here, sometimes I just
write a good tune
You provide service with poise, inside so crisp and
upholstered
The only splash of colour shines from a wooden box
now altered

You have an obsessively ordered soul with OCD
tendencies that overwhelm
Casually dressed, complete with hoodie that masks a
face, who will tell?
I've no interest in TV, I despise cinematic film
With giant bottles of coke and popcorn hot from the kiln!!

When I walked off the last time, when I trashed
everything in sight
It was kind of a cathartic move to smash and grab
throughout the night
Now I've got millions of regrets about things I've said
and done
I just wanted for you to see the scale, all I wanted was a
bit of fun!

Would you set yourself on fire? Would you carve "EVIL"
in my arms?
This is phenomenal and subversive, will you hurt me?
Will you cause me harm?
Your hand written list arrives in the post on beautiful ink
– marked paper, crisp and white
Now I feel both disconnected and excited at the
possibility of getting something right.

H.C. 24/08/2009

Suicidal Resistance

As I stand on the bridge
I take in the moment
That I want to jump in
And get washed away by the current

Then a man came alone
He was humming a song
But stopped to talk to me
To convince me that life's meant to belong

For a moment I could fly
As so uplifted by his words
But I've heard all this before
Now it all sounded so absurd

He made a grab for my hand
And pulled me until I was grounded
I know now he meant well, but
Were all my thoughts and fears founded?

Ending it all there's no return
To face a new soul's existence
Surely the next life will provide
Me with hope and peace without
"Suicidal Resistance"

H.C. 05/02/2009

Tempting Fate

Blow your brains out, leave a suicide note
Quote your favourite line of poetry as blood soaks …
Into your faded existence, better to burn out
Than to fade away, please shut your mouth!!!

You carved 'EVIL' into your arms, now bleeding
Put away the razor blade and start to focus on healing
You dredged every ounce of faith I had in humanity
My tragic fury was lost when I faced hypocrisy

Dangers of intelligence can really intimidate
Those that try to control me, I've lost the ability to
retaliate
Why only give me twenty minutes when I clearly need
an hour?
Then when you do, you resent my needs that sap your
power

With all the charisma, with all the conviction
Of someone hiding murderous revenge, you lack
manipulation
You're young and beautiful, you present like a skeleton
Then you try to run away, the exposed truth now
relevant

I expected you to get angry, start grabbing at your shins
Like the annoying twat that never smiles but grins
It was a minor detail of the day taking time out to rise to
the bait
That's dangled in front of me tempting you and tempting
fate!!

H.C.   27/03/2008

"I'm Busy

Digging Myself

Out Of A Hole

That I Think

I've Dug Myself

Into"

H.C. 10/12/2008

Troubled

I feel so troubled by everything, I'm contemplating
ending my own life
Sit with me and hold my hand, while you tell me to stay
alive
In the deepest darkness of despair, thoughts of suicide
are not chosen
It happens when pain exceeds coping with pain that just
leaves me frozen

Why do I feel so bad, crazy and weak? Flawed by
feelings of suicide
Do I really want to end it all? Do I really want to roll over
and die?
If the weight on my shoulders gets too much I will
eventually fall over and collapse
However, how much? I want to stand, just don't bring
me a cup of tea and say relax

Willpower is not a part of this course, I would try to
cheer up
We all have different tolerance levels, but for me I have
had enough
The point pain is bearable will be different to what I can
carry
Compared to how others will cope, for we all have
different levels of capacity

I cannot withstand this pain any more, it's not because
of a defect in me
It's an imbalance of pain verses coping, but my
resources have exhausted me
I need to have a sense of hope, I need the courage to
survive

I need to know others have coped with trying to stay alive

I need to put some distance between thinking and acting
Upon my suicidal tendencies, it's all the pain to which I'm reacting
Suicide is about seeking relief from all the pain and hurt
That I just can't take any more, I don't want to feel it, I'm burnt

Suicide is neither wrong or right, I have not got a defective personality
It's simply an imbalance of pain verses coping with vulnerability
I remember relief is a feeling and I have to be alive to feel it
Will I feel the relief that I seek if I am dead and I have sealed it?

H. C. 12/05/2008

Sanctuary From Suicide

Please save my life
Please believe my pain
And my suffering
Who is to blame?

Please give me sanctuary
Please hear my cries
Of suicidal urges
That make me want to die

Please give me support
And gentle surroundings
Of reflection and rest
And your understanding

Please alleviate my despair
And suicidal thoughts
Reconnect my hope
Out from being distraught

Please kill me
Before I do
Will I succeed?
Will I bleed?

Please de-stigmatise
My state of mind
That's so dark
And so unkind.

H.C. 08/03/2008

Ideas In My Head

What is my purpose in this life?
Am I special and unique?
When will I find my path?
Will I find love and be complete?

Would it really be a shame
To end my life just days...
Before I found love so strange
And recovered my own ways

Many times in our lives
Are unexpected and that means
That we often find hope and joy
When we least expect dreams

What do I do if I decide
Not to kill myself, and
The pain still hasn't gone away
What hand of cards was I dealt?

Do I have the courage to live
People are not as perceptive
As we would like to think they are
So I need to reach out and give

Maybe life is a dangerous addiction
So get yourself to a support group
And open a new door in your life
Nurture yourself and then recoup

At some point suicidals ask for help
It's not based on gender, class or race
Happiness is expressed, before
Thoughts of suicide take place

Talking of suicide can save a life
Don't be afraid to talk about death
Don't be afraid to ask how they'd do it
For it won't "plant" ideas in my head!!

H.C. 09/08/2008

Her Suicide

Please don't leave her alone
Talking about suicide can save her life
Don't be afraid to talk about death
It's comfortable to talk about her suicide

Feel free to ask her if she has a plan
Don't be afraid to ask how she'd do it
For she has already given it thought
Planning ideas in her head doesn't fit

So what is the "Weapon" of her choice?
She will keep any promise she'd made
Committing suicide sounds like a crime
Bringing about guilty feelings of blame

She thinks she needs encouragement to talk
It's okay if you feel you can't handle her legacy
Or is she just feeling misunderstood?
She has the right to claim back her sanity

Please don't leave her alone
Talking about suicide can save her life
Don't be afraid to talk about death
It's comfortable to talk about her suicide.

H.C. 11/08/2008

"When I Get On

The Right Track I

Must Refuse To Give

It Up. I Need To

Keep Going And Not

Look Back"

H.C. 23/10/2008

Feels So Cold

Do you perceive suicide
As sinful and cowardly?
For is it one's right to
Take their life if necessary?

By preventing this choice
You make them suffer more
How do we perceive ethics
When life is one big plan?

Yes, suicide it is selfish
But so are millionaires
Yes it hurts those left behind
But I question who really cares?

If one commits suicide
It's pretty high in a hundred years
No-one will know or care
About reasons and the fears

Well if I murder someone
I'll face life behind bars
If I terminate an unborn life
It's legal, but guilt goes far

It's not up to you
To decide what is
Right for me!! or even
What is right for my sanity!!!

You can try to talk
Me out of this, but
There's nothing left to hold
On to, except to dismiss

This life, that's too hard
You don't need to hold
On to my guilt that burns
Like a flame but feels so cold.

H.C. 15/08/2008

Hope I Die And Go To Heaven

Will killing myself
Totally destroy you?
Your life will never
Be the same too!

The pain you'll feel
At my own suicide
Will always stay with you
And you will wonder why

You'll hurt so much
The pain is unbearable
That I'd never imagined
For even not understandable

Is this what I wanted
For my family and friends
Did they really care?
Would they make amends?

I feel so depressed
Everything feels like shit
Suicidal thoughts consume
My being every little bit

My suicide will cause hurt
I'll reject myself if I'll live
Did I have much to live for
Throwing it all away you can't forgive...

What I'm feeling now
Will it last forever?
They say time's a healer
Hope I die and go to heaven!!

H.C. 29/08/2008

Vulnerability

He is the man
That's a paedophile
They are the ones
Whose acts are so vile

Touching and groping
To find the buttons
That when pressed
Spark off emotions...

That feel bad
That feel cold
I'm still a child
But I feel so old

Caressing brutally
To spark a reaction
Never giving up
I need a distraction

She is the woman
That has betrayed me
Along with the stress
Who stole my
Vulnerability

H.C. 26/04/2009

Move On

If I could move on
I would
If I could forget
I would

But I find it so hard
To unwind
I find it a challenge
To unwind

So I turn to drink
And learn
To escape this hell
I'll learn

I need to be fair
To myself
I need to be aware
Of myself

And of my feelings
So loaded with meanings
For all my feelings
I find so demeaning

Move on, move on
Build up one by one
Move on, move on
Under the sun, it's begun.

H.C. 27/06/2009

"The Danger Of Knowing

A Little Theology Is That

We Start Thinking We

Can Fathom The Unfathomable"

H.C. 21/08/2008

You Say You Know / What Is Faith?

You say all my days were planned, you knew my
substance in the womb
You saw me being made a secret, you never gave me a
chance to bloom
Did you see me being abused? Did you hear my childhood
terror?
Evil has descended upon me, did you know then, as my
carer?

How is it that you didn't save me? Stop all this happening
to your child
How did your faith fail to rescue me? Leaving me
abandoned in the wild
Is the fact that I am a survivor an indication of my strength?
Even though all of that terror, coming out of it to fight
what's next...

Even today, I know what I need but I can't feel my
emotions
Then tears roll down my cheeks and I feel less in isolation
Maybe some love and hope plus forgiveness and belief
In myself will speed up my recovery and get me on my feet

What is faith? What is God? Where was he in my time of
need?
That went from a day to a life, so much trauma makes me
bleed
I do not understand God's ways but I am still alive to see
God's kindness in my life, traumas of love that were a
reality

What is faith? What is love?
Shattered, exposed and all too much!!

H.C. 04/03/2009

(My) Dance Of Anger

Misdirected anger has been
A problem in my relationships
Changing the way I use my anger
For me to do has been the hardest

I've lost control over my thoughts
And emotions many times in the past
Letting my anger and frustration speak for me
Hostility to everyone seems to last

It's now painful to look back
And be reminded of all the hurt
And hateful words that came out
Of my mouth emptying all the dirt

My anger seems beyond my control
Exploding from deep inside
Confronting transforms my anger
Into sadness, full of tears I cried

I'm learning that this is a trap
One of many on my road to healing
Taking my frustration out on someone
Else just made things worse for my feelings

Inevitably feelings of regret and guilt
That followed my outbursts of anger
I would never have wanted to hurt anyone
But my anger ended up pushing up the danger

I thought I could ease the pain
By driving them away and closing off
Myself to the hurt and rejection
That I would inevitably receive enough!!!

H.C. 05/03/2009

You – Why?

You wrecked my body and you wrecked my brain
You really tried to drive me insane

You did to me what was not your right
You are the bastard of the night

You took my respect along with my pride
You have not paid for the tears I have cried

You made me hate, that I will always regret
You have not even asked for my forgiveness yet

You made me bitter and so very scared
You who my body and soul lay bare

You killed in me all the love that I had
You're not sorry and you're not even mad!

You made me hurt and badly bleed
You violated me with your obnoxious greed

You thought I was dead and you were nearly right
You did not know how for my life I would fight

You who God will punish in his own way
You will have to face your judgement day

You are so cunning and very sly
You make me sit and wonder why

H.C. 05/04/2009

The Waking Dream

A gruesome dream of hate, dead babies covered in
blood
Held by their placentas, you toss them without a look
Onto the pile they fall, screaming and slowly dying
Gasping for air and calling for their souls that are crying

From a vivid nightmare
To reality with a scream
Lost in a moment of time
To realising the waking dream...

For you removed my right, with images of hurt and pain
Every single day and night, so perverted and edging on
insane
Exhausting your daughter's body, so worn out and
buggered
Did you ever think of periods? Missed now, pregnant
you shuddered

Screwed up faces that don't smile, smothering my
thoughts so distressed
Who has the right to decide? As to whether it's kept or
destroyed
Surely it's not for you to decide, for you have a role of
responsibility
To protect your daughter's pride, instead so violated so
violently

She has to live with this legacy of immeasurable
damage and hurt
That you inflicted on one so young, not prepared or
ready to be an adult
Yet, you really didn't care for me, or for me growing
through puberty
Sexually active before her time, to meet your demands
so intolerably

From a vivid nightmare
To reality with a scream
Lost in a moment of time
To realising the waking dream.

H.C. 01/03/2009

"It's Nice To Be

Important, But

More Important

To Be Nice"

H.C. 27/11/2008

Tiananmen Square: It's Never Too Late

He quickly became an activist
Soon to organise a protest
Ready for change with a palpable sense
A student's death triggered the test

The biggest pro-democracy protest
That China had ever, ever seen
To mourn his death by marching
To Tiananmen Square, such a dream!

A dream demanding for the government
To recognise his inspiring legacy
Freedom of speech and far more
And a greater government transparency

Declared martial law, soldiers called in
Huge numbers gathered in the square
The protest resonated many in society
Blocking tanks as far as they would dare

A historic moment had been reached
Would the impossible be within our grasp?
No buses, no street police, was it safe?
Was the city safe? Not yet ready – a relapse

Running towards the street filled with noise
Soldiers shouting at civilians followed by tanks
People lying wounded on the roads of blood
So many dead bodies, I've had enough thanks

Reaching Tiananmen Square in the empty hours
Outnumbered by soldiers, tanks on three sides
They agreed to evacuate the square peacefully
Then the lights went out, the government had lied

Driven back by the soldiers with their guns
Beating people with their iron bars so full of hate
I had never imagined a government turning on its own
People, so shocked in defeat, but it's never too late.

H.C. 25/05/2009

Frail

You detect my contradictions
With a peculiar gift of mine
A grace and power about emotions
The powers of persuasions are unkind

An overwhelming personality
You are sure I don't want to fail
It's not been easy to learn
New mechanisms that don't leave me

Frail.

H.C. 18/07/2009

Without Resurrection!

I need to air my feelings
I need to air my thoughts
Where I will feel safe
Away from all this hate

How did I get there today?
Why do I still feel so alone?
Popping pills and now therapy
Don't make me feel in reality...

With myself and all my demons
Anxiety and ghosts take me over
Alcohol and drugs serve to pollute
Just like a 21 gun salute!!

In the paper you look for news
To try and achieve an equilibrium
In the help section or personal ads
Between night and day to relax

I wish I could return to my youth
And find my own spiritual direction
Without feeling guilty or hurt
Abuse free and without resurrection!

H.C. 16/08/2009

Structure And Routine

Do you view structure and routine as boring and so very
unimaginative?
When I was struggling emotionally, structure and routine
were constructive!
I faced a blank canvas every day, I waffled, feeling
confused and disconnected
Easily overwhelmed and feeling so lonely, without a
plan of action but so affected

Do I need to be intentionally structured? Would my brain
have less room to mess around
If I had a purpose or a mission to understand my life,
would I pray when I was down?
Now my brain starts to nag at me with words like "don't
do that" and "what's the point?"
I would pray for those thoughts to vanish from my head,
with God's spirit you anoint

There was a time when I scheduled to do something
every night of the week
As it was far too hard to be alone, I need to be grounded
and find my feet
If I retreated to my room, the tomb, I had to try even
harder to keep focused
Usually staying there, except trips to the fridge, all
throughout the night I feel I will burst

I'd reach a threshold of emotional pain before I could
release it and feel better
I couldn't bow out as I felt overwhelmed, I learnt to "Do
in spite of how I feel forever"
My brain is becoming more cooperative unless I'm
hungry or suffering from fear
When I'm faced with too many stressors, I return to
structure keeping myself here

I write things down, setting goals, keeping track of what
I need to do
I know how hard it is to settle down when I feel
squashed with things new
Do you view structure and routine as boring and so very
unimaginative?
When I was struggling emotionally, structure and routine
were constructive!

H.C. 16/08/2009

"You Eat Life

Or

Life Eats You"

H.C. 20/01/2009

Helen Care

Like A Drink Spiked!

Such a lyrical retardation
Where there's no depth of soul
I have the dark heart of someone
Who couldn't take on any role

Maybe it's because up until now
I've never experienced a recession
After many years of consumerism
The harsh realities kick off a depression

There needs to be an amnesty
Where you hand in instruments
That have polluted this country
With dreadful and average decadence

It's totally unrecognisable
To the world you left behind
It's such a catastrophic change
The internet has been such a friend

People think they're really informed
They're popular with lots of "friends"
They're part of the community
They have a voice they want to lend...

But they don't realise, like all of us
They're completely fucked and powerless
An unbelievable misconception of self
It's all about self-ism and willingness

I grew up thinking I should be unpopular
And that I should definitely be disliked
There's no integrity, just fake
Intellectually, like a drink spiked!

H.C. 24/08/2009

You Just Don't Get It!

I've just dealt with all that stuff
I don't need closure or confirmation
I don't know how I've made this decision
Maybe through persuasion and humiliation

And if you're dead in my future
I really think I'd handle it
Here in the reality of today
Centred on flaming love like this

There's always something eating
Away at me, like a hole
The trick is to keep like this
Otherwise consumption takes its toll

The bitterness and the anger
Took over and devoured me
I'm too awkward and complicated
To understand my own reality

My politics are confused
My attitude out-of-sync
Unless you lived it
You just don't get it!

H.C. 24/08/2009

Red Light

You crawl up my wall
And invade my privacy
Cockroach of the gutter
And life of depravity

Sometimes a red light
Tells you to stop
Pick up a calling card
In the phone box

I slink through alleyways
Avoiding the law
You love me, you loathe me
You watch me in awe

Bleeding lines
Drawn with a knife
I lick my wounds
This is my life

Money makes the
World go round
Here's my flesh
Now take your pound

Sometimes a red light
Tells you to stop
Perhaps I should slow
Down before I get too hot!

H.C. 06/04/2009

Get Off The Fence

Whatever we do, we can't leave them here
In this dangerous street, the children need action, not a tear!
Today, when even the thought of children playing on the street
Can be alarming, imagine what life is like for a child that's beat...

A child that's forced on the pavement to live in one of the poor locations
Children living alone and unprotected, they need to be rescued from this situation
For the abandoned child on the street being hungry, thirsty, cold
Unwashed is part of their daily life, your offer of support is a step so bold

They're exposed to all kinds of dangers, exploitation and physical violence
Child labour and much trafficking, paedophiles pounce to pack a punched clench
On the street, children from a very young age have to fend and fight for themselves
And with a lack of love and security of a family life they exist in their own hell

Children need someone to be there for them, such stability, structure and a sense
Of belonging, gives hope and kindness to a child that needs you to get off the fence!!
Whatever we do, we can't leave them here
In this dangerous street, they need action, not a tear!!

H.C. 25/05/2009

> "I Have No Plan,
>
> No Attention Span
>
> And Very Little Focus.
>
> I Guess I'll Just
>
> Make It Up As I Go
>
> Along"

H. C. 07/01/2009

A Celebration?

Life should be a celebration
Full of hope, joy and recovery
There should be no blame
But it is inherent in my destiny

Call me lost in the desert
Parched enough to search
For an oasis that never
Appears to quench my thirst

Did I choose to be sick
In order to become well?
What a ridiculous comment
My recovery is under your spell

The water I have drunk
Has brought me restoration
The medical world falters
When hope promises exhilaration

This I really longed for
Difficult people, same journey
A small girl, now a woman
Aware of her inner beauty

H.C. 29/03/2008

Feeling The Feelings

Sometimes I can't believe
We're "civilised human beings"
Having no other option to establish
Global peace feeling the feelings

Through the same old centuries
Were our primitive ancestors
Used to solving their conflicts
With violence; this was their answer

But we have enlarged our minds
To comprehend that we are a clot
In our galaxy in the vast
Universe which is also a blot

It goes beyond our perception
If we could broaden our minds
To see far into the galaxies
To see deep into us – mankind

Of which we are composed
So why have we failed in our compassion
In our hearts to understand that
The same path is not just a fashion

This pain we're inflicting on others
Just like the beat of rhythm
In nature's circle so primitive
And barbarian name by way of a solution

We try to solve our conflicts
With brutal force of destruction
We spin around and around like madmen
In a vicious circle of anger and frustration

Sometimes I can't believe
We were "civilised human beings"
Having no other option to establish
Global peace feeling the feelings

H.C. 23/08/2008

God And Suffering

There are so many people
Who've stopped believing in God
As they see the despair of mankind
Blaming God for us suffering a lot

Nothing will happen before it's time
There's a time for war, and
There's a time for peace
But no love for us all

We're in the process of shifting
Gears from eternal wars
To genuine everlasting peace
But as individuals, we're the cause

Which choice will they make?
One for world peace, or a
Habitual ignorance to wake up
And go along with empty release

Will we change our old beliefs?
Or will we cling to our comfort zone?
Even though we don't get happiness
That's real and one we can condone

If we don't change our course
Our world will remain the same
Old chaos and then one day
One world will absorb our blame

The world will be torn apart
By incredible destructive forces
Facing such unbearable panic
Then it will be too late for pauses

There are so many people
Who've stopped believing in God
As they see the despair of mankind
Blaming God for us suffering a lot.

H.C. 23/08/2008

The Way Up When Life Gets You Down

There are times in life
When we all feel down
Please show me the way
As I'm going round and round

I didn't start off in the doldrums
I didn't start off the fire ball
That lit up the skies of heaven
Wake up and God will call

False prophets versus Guardian Angels
All face a multitude of evil
Fear makes us forget their power
A skewered perspective so suicidal

Exhaustion with fear is dangerous
A fateful combination that's hopeless
And wrong thinking, and so creates
The illusion that I am careless...

When I most need your support
Anxiety and inadequacy put me
Into fear of failure and isolation
I'm on my own when I need your company

It may be bad now and
I can't see it getting better
When I feel so down and low
It isn't time to isolate and get her!

I need to reach out
To the people that love me
Who can help me back up
Out of my dark soul that weeps

Please give me the prescription
For getting back on my feet
I've had no rest or nourishment
No wonder I don't feel complete.

H. C.   03/09/2008

"We Need To Create

A World Where All

People Are Safe,

Accepted And Supported,

Where They Feel Loved

And Respected"

H.C. 06/01/2009

No Solace

A solitary road
I take, I must
No one to turn to
No one to trust

You've condemned me
By words you fed
The longest path
That I can tread

My lips be sealed
Pain and angst so cold
Kept locked within
Deep within my soul

No harm extended
For a final sigh
No one to shame
My last goodbye.

H.C. 06/04/2009

Searching

Emotional instability
Severe doubts about
My self image and soul
That make me shut my mouth

Sexual preferences
Cause upset and distress
A strong and debilitating
Sense of emptiness...

Can lead to self harm
And suicidal ideation
Such intense and unstable
Relationships lead to isolation

Continual emotional crisis
Which will be endured
To avoid being abandoned
Still searching for a cure!!

H.C. 10/06/2009

Need To Be

The evidence is indisputable
Outspoken, unashamed
Out of control and staggering
From the brink of blame

Back from disaster to success
Then back to mayhem and madness
Ignored for all her transgressions
That hailed her brave no less

Damaged looks, scars to match
Living on such a rollercoaster
Nearly destroyed along the way
Sex, alcohol, drugs connect her...

Love is not lost
She has been
Fat, broke and
Stoned in between

Now she is remade and
Remodelled, just
Need to be stoned
And untroubled

No more substances, so
Please take her seriously
She can't fake it, just can't
This leaves her laughing deliriously

She is open about her life
A sorry spiral of loss and pain
A childhood of destruction
She couldn't bear the same

Everything she loved
Has been taken away
But she still has more to give
She apologises once again!!

H.C. 27/12/2008

That Biz Again!!!

So sad
Am I mad?
Get high
In this life

So down
For a clown
Shed a tear
Feel the fear

Go fast
Will it last?
Sniff the wiz
Just the biz

Go slow
Blow by blow
Take the pain
Again and again

Sad, down, fast then slow
Mad, clown, last, by blow
High, tear, wiz, the pain
Life of fear, that biz again!!!

H.C. 05/01/2009

"How Can We Find

The Way To The Door

Of Inner Happiness

That Can Lead Us

Into The Light Of

Healing?"

H.C. 08/02/2009

In Crisis

I'm not looking for arrogance
I just want to come out and escape
I'm not looking for intimidation
There's so much anger and hate

I need to turn this venom
Into poetry, music and art
Then I will be dead
Due to my very toxic heart

I wish I was a grounded girl
I wish I was beautifully raised
I never had the desire to be
Someone who got through this phase

Please don't hate me
In the way you should
I knew I wasn't cool
In the way that I could

Having a conversation with you
Is part of laughter and gossip
Telling an unprintable tale
Where you become your hardest critic

Such charming and compelling company
You are the centre of attention
For you have significant presence
Even on your best behaviour with no tension

Your personality spills out on the floor
From an oversized bag of hope
At the height of your disorderly conduct
I pray for indifference and the ability to cope

I'll occasionally forget my words
My life needs to be furnished
To add comfort and security
To my existence that's in crisis.

H.C. 06/01/2009

Blame

It takes all my time
To stand on my own two feet
I can't afford to fall overboard
For I have to live and sleep

Hope can be so dangerous
It can get you crucified
It can get you misunderstood
For I have to learn how to cry

However I don't feel ready
My life needs to be sorted
Then I'll have something to offer
For I have bought it

I am so afraid
That I'll let you down
What will you think me?
I am weak and I frown

My spirit has been destroyed
By the surgeon who operated
To remove the wrong body part
Self inflicted injuries leave me frustrated

Holding hope for someone
Who can't hold it themselves
They need knowledge and a belief
That they have the capacity for help

Angry, upset and scared
Fuzzy seeds of harm
Take a chance and smile
And then try to stay calm

I am afraid
That I'll fail to sustain
My determination and hope
Am I the one to blame?

H.C. 21/06/2008

Conquer

My mouth is dry
My palms are wet
My head is spinning
I can't talk as yet

Put my head down
Build your character
Seek the truth
What does it matter?

Learn all you can
To teach and heal
From mercy to grace
It needs to be real

Do not be afraid
As you will survive
Come out in the open
Conquer all their lies.

H. C. 05/07/2008

The Allure Of A Hero

It feels mildly sacrilegious
Just to sit on the chair
Like sitting on the throne
Like God without a care!

He looks at the chair
Changes it for something new
For the moment is over
Go to the back of the queue!

This is a displacement activity
Why are you bored and nervous?
There are only a few seconds
No margin for error, you're anxious!

No space to tell someone
They've got food in their teeth
Such inhospitable hospitality
Now drinking lukewarm tea

More people drift into
The dark corners of the room
Wearing sleek shoes and silk ties
The fashion police can't come too soon

They are the captains of consumption
They hold a small memento
A religious image to be displayed
Discreetly find a place to go

Not used to being kept waiting
But before you meet your hero
In this topsy-turvy world of clarity!
Celebrities need to take a blow...

To the bottom of the cheek bone
Arm clasping, back stabbing
The talent comes first and then
The rest of us are left just gasping

What keeps us all on the go
Is the allure of a hero.

H.C. 17/08/2008

"The Pain Of Understanding

And Healing I Hope Will

Be Far Less Than The Pain

Of Denial And Despair"

H.C. 03/03/2009

On The Road To Recovery

Mental health problems develop because bad things
can happen
The mind retains information, transformed, disguised
and forgotten
For the pain has to be bearded and the horrors
remembered
You can feel so alone you want to feel brutally severed

Listening is difficult, accept the feelings
Accept the truth that is revealing
An emotional resonance, an empathic response
Feeling heard and understood, smile so you don't get
lost!

Accept you as you are, not focusing on the negative
Is there something wrong? Will your criticism ever
forgive?
The person is as good as they are, providing grounds
for hope
Try to recover what you lost, don't hang yourself with
rope

You can make do with putting together a series of
relationships
But if they're damaged and broken, repetition of
mistakes is shit!
"Yes, they will do that for me, which may mean I am
worth it"
Back on the road to recovery, stone by stone, brick by
brick.

H.C. 06/01/2009

Tears, That's Okay!

I am shown to the room
With the flowered sheet
I can't feel my feet, and
My thoughts are full of doom

I imagine a golden light
And draw energy from the earth
That I've had since my birth
But it's out of mind, out of sight

From the base of my spine
I can feel a cord to the ground
The pin drops without a sound
I sew up my thoughts, it takes time

Feelings don't go away
Put them in storage to think
While I engage, but sink
In my tears, that's okay!

H.C. 17/01/2009

Reaching Up Again

I can't hold onto my healing
It slips through my fingers
So that I'm locked inside myself
Without a solution that lingers

The rest of my life comforts me
Tears of sarcasm are critical
Why do I see others and not me
When I need to focus on my survival?

Where does the calm feeling go
When I feel at ease, supported?
There are many feelings as diverse
As the seasons and oceans are perverted

But it seems like my pain was stolen
My pleasant feelings putting them
Into a bundle for short glimpses
Like a child reaching up again.

H.C. 17/01/2009

My Fantasy

Pain steals pleasant feelings, tying them into a bundle
I feel like a child reaching up with no chair, I stumble
Dreams and plans for my future just seem increasingly
impossible
Inside I'm in a room that's empty, suicide fantasies are
so incredible!

They're like a death movie in my mind, my arms ache
with wanting to touch
They fill up the air waiting to be picked up, death is far
too much
I wish someone would take care of me and show me
what to say and do
How do I get what I've never had? My thirst for love
feels so overdue.

When does neediness become a burden? I hold my
breath and then I hope
You won't notice the grasping hands inside of me trying
to elope
But when the touch is gone, the need for assurance
comes back
As if there had never been any touch at all, something
that I lack

I pace back and forth frantically, I can't handle another
minute
I just keep feeling like dying, sorry to keep telling you
this

I want to jump out of the window or stick my head in the
oven
Words tumble out in pools of tears that I drown in quite
often

Everything is moving too fast
I want you to hold me
To stop me from feeling sad
Don't let go of my fantasy.

H.C. 18/01/2009

"We Are All Caterpillars

Making Our Cocoons

And Soon We Will Be

Beautiful Butterflies

Ready To Fly Away"

H.C. 07/06/2009

"Look At Me"

"Look at me"
While I lower my head
Isn't it time
That I took you to bed?

"Look at me"
While we both play
Our games
Please go away

"Look at me"
While I feel and touch
You're touching me
This is far too much

"Look at me"
Please make them happy
Look at me
No, don't look at me!!

H.C. 11/12/2007

Until I Can No Longer Pretend

You know that awful feeling
In the pit of your stomach
When you know for sure that
It's all over, you've run out of luck

Your loved one is walking away
Walking off into the sunset
You're left to pick up the pieces
Of your life and rebuild the wreck

This hasn't come as a relief
But as the worst heartbreak
That I could ever imagine
It just makes my heart ache

So how do you bounce back
From losing someone in your life?
Faced with a big hole of loss
A reaction of shock creates strife

I need to have time to be sad
For this is a recognisable sense
I need time to be so angry
Until I can no longer pretend.

H.C. 08/05/2008

Far Too Late

I can feel your affection
I can still feel your touch
Which now feels like rejection
Which now feels far too much

I can hear your laughter
With the sunshine in your smile
I can listen to your adventures
That captivate me for miles

I can feel your hugs of love
I can breathe in your energy
Fill both my body and soul
These thoughts I feel affectionately

I want to hug you back
I want to touch your face
But soon you will be gone
And then it will be far too late.

H.C. 17/05/2008

"Bleed Her Dry"

Extremely high maintenance
Just to get a laugh out of you
Manipulative and disruptive
She wants you to worry about her too!

Make her behave and really listen
For she responds well to your hope
In her, she frequently loses sight
You are her compass for her to cope

She sits down overwhelmed by tears
She is plump but very unique
She strives to gain maturity
She has it all within, she's not weak

She is always on the lookout
For some distress to kick start
Something to give her a headache
All her songs come from her heart

Back into a dark place of
Mood swings and drunken binges
Prompting rebounded and creative
Verses that say it like it is

She is just as switched on
As of fifteen years previously
Pouring out of her like a
Tidal wave so fiercely

Her free fall into addiction
Was more like her best friend
Keeping her feet on the ground
Her search for peace will never end

She certainly won't listen to you
Shenanigans prompt her to flee
From this rat-race of emotions
That "bleed her dry" effortlessly.

H.C. 16/08/2008

"Angels Exist But,

Sometimes, Since They

Don't All Have Wings

We Call Them Friends"

H.C. 22/02/2009

Tempt Me With Treasure

Sometimes I feel happy
And next I'm going mad
I feel I always have to perform
Now I'm exhausted and feeling sad

Inside I feel I'm dying
What is the right way
To overcome my emotions
That plague my day?

I used to have a healthy mind
Even though I felt so down
I find it hard to come to terms
With issues that make me frown

I've turned to books and music
To find another way to give
I've stopped trusting my own instinct
I'm so angry with myself, but I'll live

I feel like an emotional wreck
I'm trying to find some pleasure
In normal day-to-day things
That tempt me with treasure.

H.C. 30/08/2008

Rehabilitation

Bit by bit, my wounds
Will start to heal
The scars are still there
But I soon can feel

I will stop asking myself why
Or beating myself up
I try to understand why
It happened and why I cut

I start to think about
How my life will pan out
And what the future holds
It'll be difficult I don't doubt

I hope my desires will return
And the inquisitiveness shines
Allowing me to discover new things
That are there to be kind

Hopefully life will suddenly
Seem sweet again, and
Welcome me with open arms
Embracing my fears and pain.

H.C. 30/08/2009

When Trust Is Lost

When trust is lost
At whatever cost...

Left with feelings of powerlessness
Left with a feeling of betrayal
Left with a feeling of confusion
Being rejected by a God in denial

I need to find hope by facing the truth
Finding comfort by embracing sorrow
Finding peace by choosing to surrender
Finding joy and love that's not hollow

It has brought me much shame
I have lost my innocence and self respect
Silenced so that help was hard to find
The wounds and struggles have an effect...

And are often difficult to deal with
I feel so alone, depressed and confused
I feel out of control and losing my mind
At all these times I was used and abused

When trust is lost
At whatever cost...

H.C. 03/03/2009

Double The Stigma

Anxiety, sadness and irritability
A lack of support and vulnerability
A lack of understanding for this depression
That overwhelms me like a confession

Attribute my symptoms to difficulties of living
The stigma attached is never forgiving
I need more understanding, more empathy and support
For my needs are daunting as my soul has been bought

I feel like I'm somebody else, even though I appear to
be fine
I'm stupid, careless and dirty, where do you draw the
line?
I'm experiencing suicidal distress, I feel so alone and
isolated
I'm confused, my head bombarded with filth that I have
contemplated

An illness with no visible signs, don't stop stigma to
underline
My existence that's medically managed, too many pills
makes me feel sublime
People don't want to get involved, such rejection only
serves to feed
My anger that leaves me depressed, my comfort zone is
where I concede

Anxiety, sadness, irritability
A lack of support and vulnerability
A lack of understanding for this depression
That overwhelms me like a confession.

H.C. 20/12/2008

"Forgiveness Is The

Giving Up Of Resentment"

H.C. 31/03/2009

Helen Care

Thinking On My Feet

I woke up with a start, they had come for me
As I knew they would – this was my reality
Watch my stomach exhale as I get up and get dressed
In the silence and in the dark leave the warmth and
confess

Get out without them knowing, or do I accept what's
happening?
The clock radio sounds strange, picking up the sound of
my collapsing
My heart thumps, my mouth is dry, I act cool and calm,
my saving grace
I can't let you know, I'm afraid, I guess I'll die with your
hate

They are moving in fast, I'm thinking on my feet
Fight the need to concede, by thinking on my feet

Bring me a drink, I will swallow. It's poisoned, but I don't
suspect a thing
I listen to you, but I don't understand these changes that
you always bring
I tried to escape without being spotted, we struggled
and wiggled some more
I was scared, would they let me go? There is nowhere
safe, don't close the door!

I don't try to run, it's futile, I'm surrounded by so many
violators
Telling me that I would be incinerated if I knew too much
to be a survivor
Perhaps poisoning would be a preferable method to die
Then they won't get their hands over me, I need to cry

They are moving away, I'm thinking on my feet
Even though I am stuck, I am thinking on my feet.

H.C. 07/11/2008

Like Nothing Else

I know the suffering
That anger can inflict
It's such a stumbling block
To my personality being fixed

Although I often felt angry
I quickly stifled angry feelings
Because I felt scared of them
They weren't openly appealing

I started to believe
I was the incredible hulk
The most angry person around
Left only on my own to sulk

Since no-one seemed to speak
About or openly express
Their feelings of anger
No more, No less!!

First my anger wasn't explosive
It was a force that was implosive
Turning my anger in on myself
Depression and self harm like nothing else!

H.C. 16/11/2008

The Tree Of Eyes

You're always looking on the bright side
But it's fucking dark and creepy
Every time I look around in here
All I see are these cold walls so deeply

I've been in this darkness for a long time
The trees bare their branches like skeletons
Losing my flesh, my mouth carries
The light plastic smile she insisted on

The smile was a lie required
And now I can't seem to take it off
I walk a zigzag path around puddles
Waiting for quicksand is quite enough

I pause in front of a large tree
I throw my arms around its trunk
When I close my eyes I feel calm
A welcome change from feeling drunk

My shoulders relax for now
I want to feel the cold air
Climb deeper into my soul
Is this the right way to declare?

As the bottom of my feet tingle
I imagine sinking below the tree
My legs grow past its roots
I draw my breath and feel free

Being grounded is like meeting the Earth
Accepting the support of being held upright
Quit daydreaming of discrediting my thoughts
I do belong here whether that's wrong or right

The more I explore my inner world
The more I notice, even when my eyes
Are open to this peculiar vision
The more I understand, then the more I feel alive

Helen Care 20/12/2008

Touch

Please place your hands
On my heart and soul,
So my fingers will curl over
From your warmth that's not cold

I wish I could be an open channel
For loving and healing energy
Moving right through my body
Exhaling and breathing in harmony

I imagine an ocean
Gushing right through me
It's so vast and so deep
Holding life, the tide and sea

Then I hope my body
For this very first time
Will be filled with TOUCH
That's so loving and kind.

H.C. 17/01/2009

"Everything Should

Come From The Heart

Love Is The Most

Powerful Drug Of All"

H.C. 07/01/2009

Jesus Will Leave Me Alone

I'm in a state of shock
I'm in a state of disbelief
Maybe I should be a philosopher
Thinking over what could've been

I feel so uncomfortable
I feel so different
I feel so nervous
I lack being confident

You sounded remorseful
You tried to be reflective
Don't sound so disappointed
When you ask for my forgiveness

Maybe I should go to church
Maybe I should say my prayers
Maybe I will burn in hell
Maybe I really don't care

Maybe, I should leave Jesus alone
Maybe, Jesus will leave me alone.

H.C. 08/04/2009

Suicide, Life, Happiness, Depression

Suicide
You can't avoid
The pain it hides
Leaves me annoyed

Life
You can't breathe
With all the pain
There is no relief

Happiness
Is such a laugh
When you feel down
Don't take a photograph

Depression
Pollutes my brain
Which is worse
Being hurt or insane?

H.C. 08/05/2009

Life Out Of Love

I was grateful
I was so loyal
But not beholding
You, I did spoil

Patterns established
You know I was afraid
Our feelings collided
Knowing and believing aren't the same

When you know one thing
And believe in another
You experience conflict
With a pillow you did smother

The life out of me
The love out of me
Will I ever recover?
Will I ever find peace?

Hurt has surfaced
Anger has subsided
Love has disappeared
Emotions collided

Healing will take place
From the inside out
To the depth of my soul
I open up my mouth

Have I prayed enough?
Have I kept my faith?
Have I grown up enough?
So please don't suffocate

The life out of me
The love out of me
Will I ever recover?
Will I ever find peace?

H.C. 29/06/2008

www.ingramcontent.com/pod-product-compliance
Lightning Source LLC
Chambersburg PA
CBHW031218270326
41931CB00006B/601